MW01131802

For Bella, Elsie, and Clara, my brilliant nieces.

– Helen

For my beloved family and best friend Jun Cen.

– Lisk

First paperback edition published in 2023 by Flying Eye Books.

First published in 2021 by Flying Eye Books Ltd. 27 Westgate Street, London, E8 3RL.

Text © Helen Scales 2021
Illustrations © Lisk Feng 2021

Lisk Feng and Helen Scales have asserted their right under the Copyright, Designs and Patents Act, 1988, to be identified as the Illustrator and Author of this Work.

All rights reserved. No part of this publication may be reproduced or transmitted in any form or by any means, electronic or mechanical, including photocopying, recording or by any information and storage retrieval system, without prior written consent from the publisher.

Every attempt has been made to ensure any statements written as fact have been checked to the best of our abilities. However, we are still human, thankfully, and occasionally little mistakes may crop up. Should you spot any errors, please email info@nobrow.net.

1 3 5 7 9 10 8 6 4 2

Printed in the US by Flying Eye Books Ltd.

Printed in Poland on FSC® certified paper.

ISBN: 978-1-83874-870-8

www.flyingeyebooks.com

HELEN SCALES          LISK FENG

# THE GREAT
# BARRIER REEF

FLYING EYE BOOKS

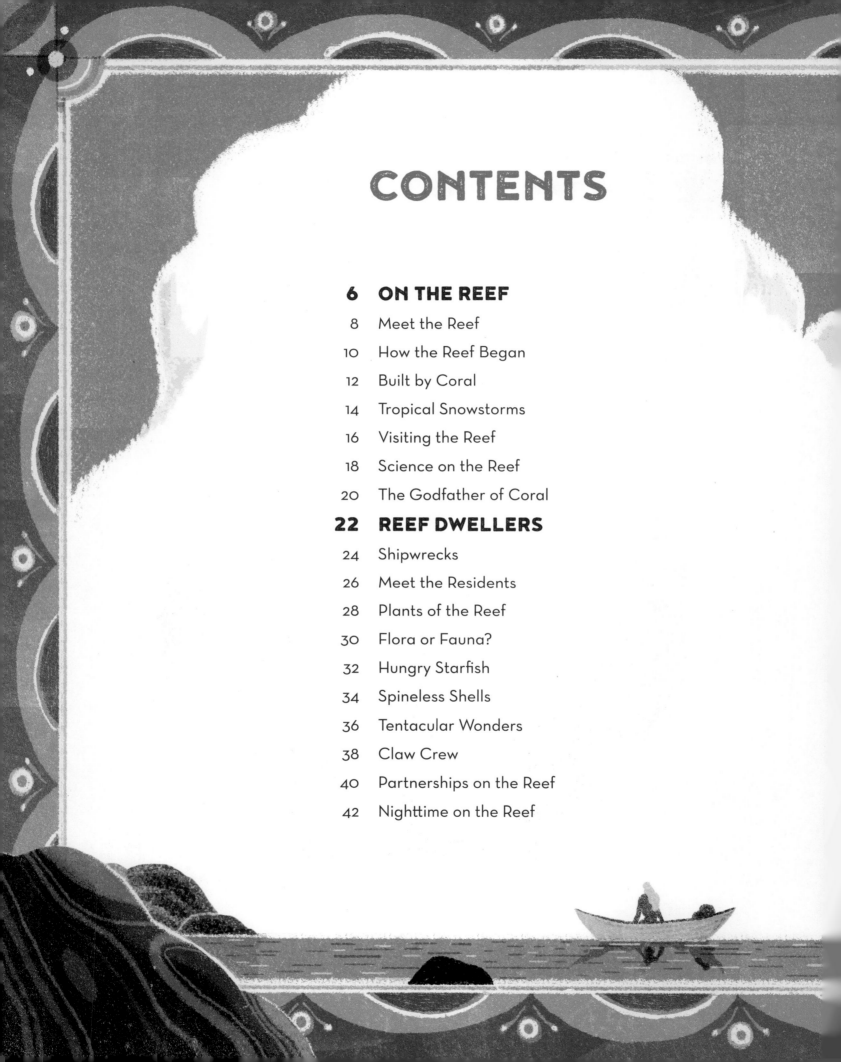

# CONTENTS

# INTRODUCTION

This is a story about one of the greatest natural wonders of the world. An underwater wonder, it is a place of breathtaking beauty, bursting with color and teeming with life. But it is a place as fragile as it is magnificent.

This is the story of the Great Barrier Reef.

# ON THE REEF

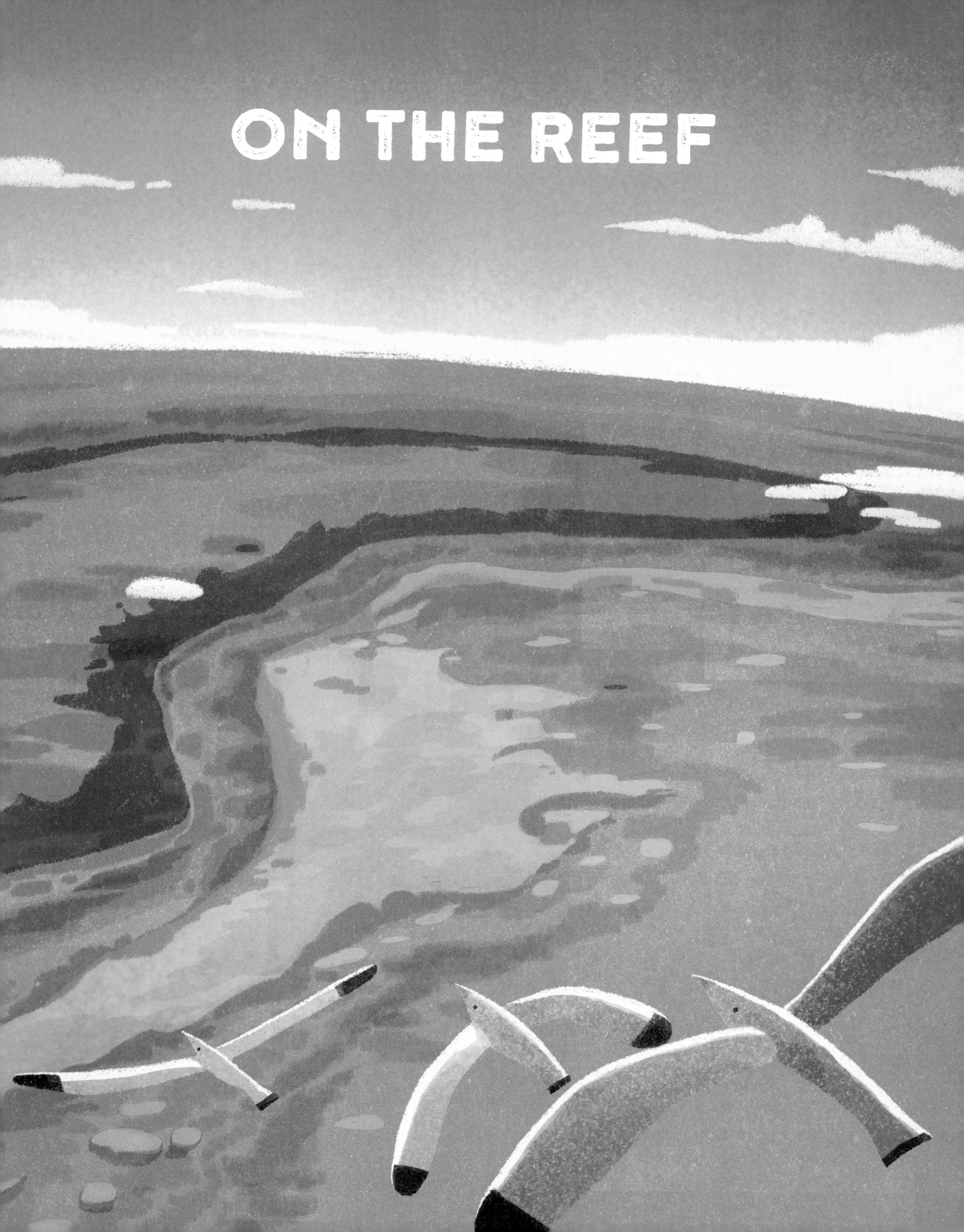

# MEET THE REEF

The Great Barrier Reef is the world's biggest coral reef system, stretching for more than 1,400 miles along Australia's coast, and covering an area the size of 70 million soccer fields. If you set out to walk that same distance it would take you three weeks, and that's without stopping to eat or take naps! Along its great length are islands of gleaming white sand fringed in green mangrove forests, and winding ribbons of reef.

The Great Barrier Reef is also a World Heritage Site.
These precious sites around the world are chosen because they
are amazing places that need to be treasured and protected.

# HOW THE REEF BEGAN

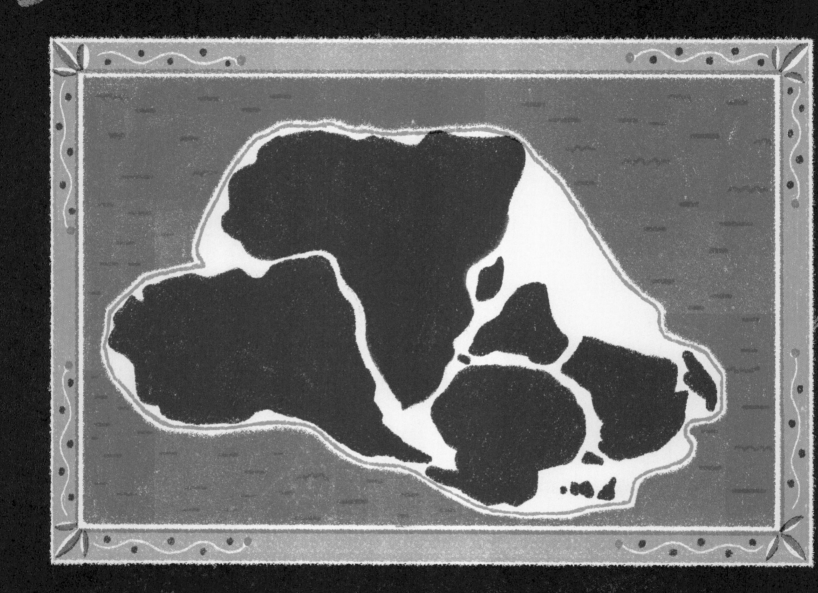

A long time ago, Australia was not the sort of place where a reef could grow. Stuck to Antarctica, it was surrounded by a freezing sea—far too cold for corals!

Then, 85 million years ago (when dinosaurs were still alive), Australia split off and began to drift away towards the equator, closer to where it is today. At this time in history the Earth was very cold. Enormous ice sheets locked up masses of the ocean's water, so sea levels were more than 300 feet lower than they are now.

Then, as the last ice age ended around 10,000 years ago, the world warmed up and the ice sheets melted, causing an enormous flood. As sea levels rose higher and higher, great cliffs disappeared beneath the waves, and hills were turned into islands. Tiny, young corals called **larvae** drifted in from other reefs and settled on this land that was suddenly underwater. The sea became warm enough for corals to thrive, and so the Great Barrier Reef began to grow. As the seas rose higher, some of the islands drowned completely, but the corals kept growing upwards and outwards until they built wide, flat reefs.

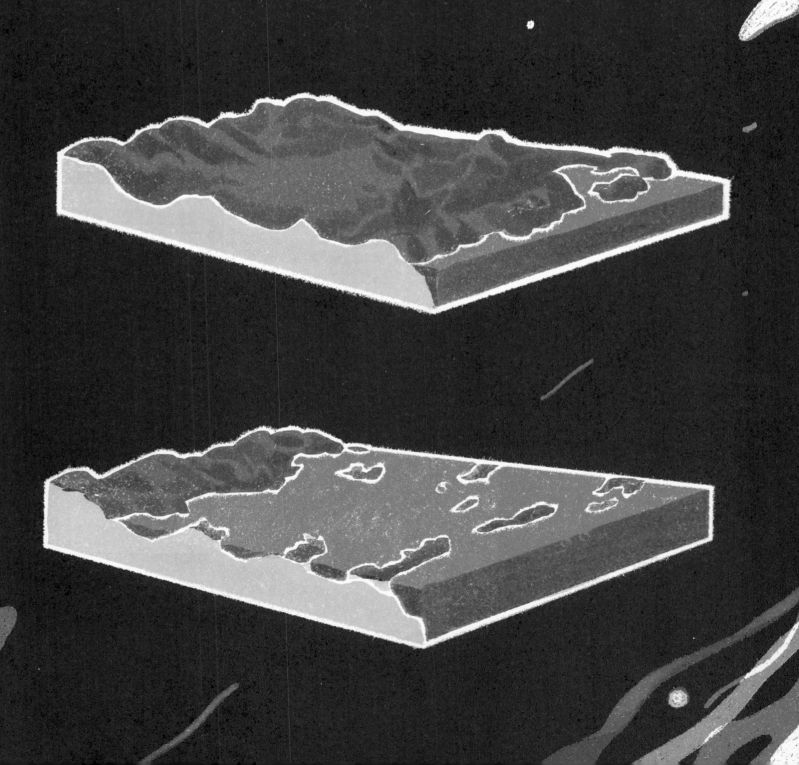

# BUILT BY CORAL

More than 600 species of corals live on the Great Barrier Reef. If you were to look closely at a piece of coral, you'll see that it's covered in spots. These are **polyps**: each one is a tiny coral animal with a mouth, a stomach, and tentacles. Coral polyps don't have brains, much like their closest relatives, jellyfish and anemones. Each big coral, known as a colony, is made up of hundreds and thousands of polyps joined together. Their bodies are soft but usually they live inside a tough **exoskeleton** made of calcium carbonate, the same stuff as chalk and chickens' eggshells.

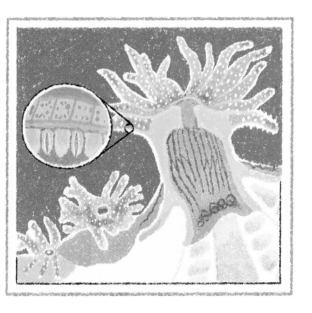

## TINY SECRETS

With the help of a **microscope** you can discover one of the polyps' hidden secrets—inside their bodies are spherical cells, called **zooxanthellae** or zoox for short. Zoox use the sun's energy to make sugar, just like plants do on land. During the day, corals eat this sugar. At night they transform into deadly hunters, using their tentacles to catch tiny animals and plant-like organisms called **plankton**. Some plankton grow into bigger animals, like fish and crabs, and some never get any bigger.

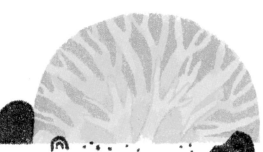

*Branching coral*

*Sea whip*

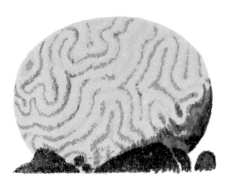

*Brain coral*

There are two different types of coral—soft and hard.
Corals with a tough exoskeleton are known as hard corals.
Corals without a hard skeleton are called soft corals.

*Elephant ear leather coral*

*Mushroom coral*

# TROPICAL SNOWSTORMS

Once a year, the Great Barrier Reef turns into a giant underwater snow globe. . . except the little snowflakes twirling about are actually millions of colorful coral eggs. The corals release them at exactly the same time. This is one way that corals can multiply and spread to new places in the ocean.

## DRIFTING LARVAE

Fertilized coral eggs hatch into larvae that look like tiny, squashed grains of rice. They are brilliant travelers, drifting for weeks on long, dangerous journeys. Many get eaten by fish along the way, but the lucky survivors will eventually settle down on rocks or pieces of dead coral, and form a brand new coral colony.

# VISITING THE REEF

People come from all over the world to visit the Great Barrier Reef. It can be seen from a glass-bottomed boat, or you can even dive right in—all you need is a diving mask, a snorkel, and perhaps a pair of flippers.

## RULES OF THE REEF

To help look after the reef, and yourself, the golden rule is not to touch anything. Some animals might sting you, and all the reef's creatures prefer not to be poked. As the saying goes, "take only memories, leave only bubbles."

## A SAFE PASSAGE

The English captain Matthew Flinders was the first to map the Australian coastline. He was also the first to describe the underwater labyrinth as a "great barrier reef," giving the reef its name. Between 1801 and 1803 he successfully navigated his way through the reef and even today "Flinders Passage" guides ships through the rocky coral.

# SCUBA DIVING

Diving with self-contained underwater breathing apparatus (SCUBA) is the closest you can get to being a fish. Before you can dive, you need to learn how to use the equipment and go on a course to obtain a diving certification. A scuba dive usually lasts between one and two hours.

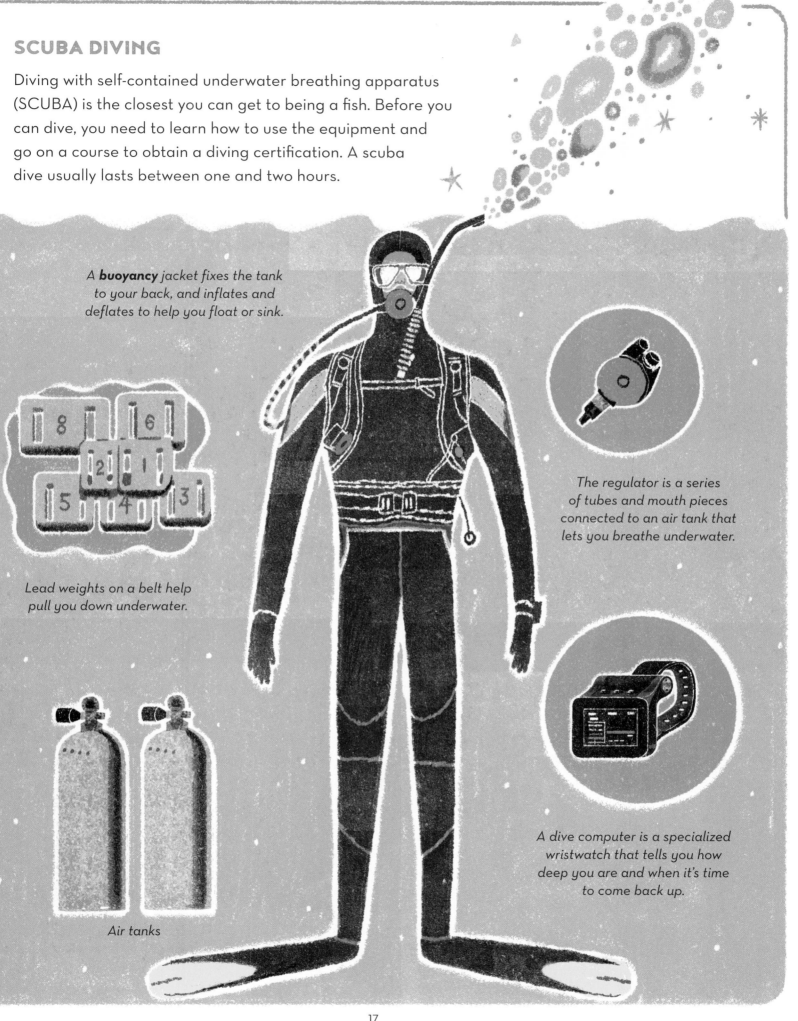

A **buoyancy** jacket fixes the tank to your back, and inflates and deflates to help you float or sink.

Lead weights on a belt help pull you down underwater.

The regulator is a series of tubes and mouth pieces connected to an air tank that lets you breathe underwater.

Air tanks

A dive computer is a specialized wristwatch that tells you how deep you are and when it's time to come back up.

17

# SCIENCE ON THE REEF

Scientists are frequent visitors to the reef. Several islands have research bases on them, and scientists can live there for weeks, months, or even years at a time. This lets them revisit the same spots day and night, getting to know the reef better than ever, and making lots of amazing discoveries.

## BELOW THE SURFACE

Scientists are now diving deeper and longer than ever before with new equipment that lets divers rebreathe the same air again and again. The equipment absorbs the carbon dioxide as the divers breathe out and adds more **oxygen** from a small tank. This lets divers go 300 feet underwater for five hours at a time.

*This type of diving does not produce any bubbles! Scientists can swim right up to fish without disturbing the water.*

## UNDERWATER ROBOTS

To look even deeper into the water, scientists lower remote-controlled robots with cameras attached. These robots have shown us that corals grow on the Great Barrier Reef much deeper than anyone realized before—down to 410 feet—where there's just enough light to keep the zoox in the coral alive.

## SEEING WITH SOUND

To study the very deepest parts of the reef, scientists use **echolocation**, just like whales and dolphins. Scientists use **sonar** machines and powerful computers to do this, creating detailed 3D maps of ocean depths.

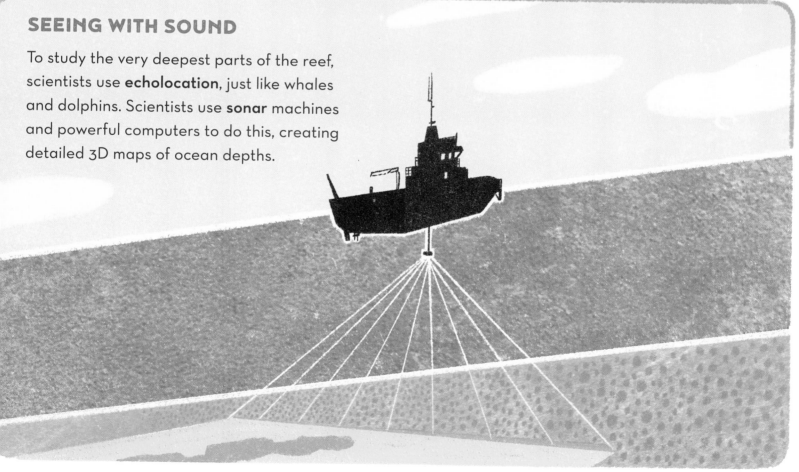

# THE GODFATHER OF CORAL

John Veron has spent almost his whole life underwater. When he was at school, one of his teachers saw how much he loved nature and called him Charlie, after the father of evolution, Charles Darwin. It was a name that stuck.

After learning to dive at 18, Charlie went on to become a specialist in the study of coral reefs and he got a job as the first full-time scientist on the Great Barrier Reef. Now in his seventies, he is still diving.

Nicknamed the "Godfather of Coral," Charlie has discovered and identified 20% of the world's coral species—more than anyone else in history. He was also one of the earliest to document **coral bleaching**, and took the world's first known photograph of a "strange white coral." At the time he didn't know why the coral was sick. Later on it was identified as suffering from coral bleaching.

Charlie is now very worried about the future of the reef and wants as many people as possible to care about it and help protect it.

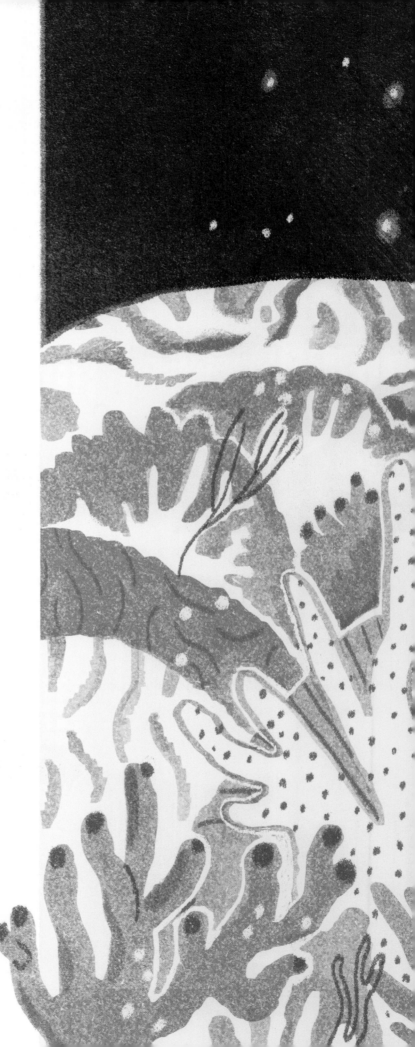

# REEF DWELLERS

# SHIPWRECKS

The Great Barrier Reef is the watery grave for more than 800 shipwrecks. Some of them crashed into the reef and sank. Some were lost during storms. As they lie on the seabed, the wrecks become covered in colorful sea life and turn into reefs themselves.

The reef's most famous shipwreck is the *SS Yongala*. It was a steam ship powered by coal and it carried passengers and cargo along Australia's coasts over a hundred years ago. Tragedy struck on March 23rd, 1911. There was a terrible storm and the *SS Yongala* sank to the seabed. All 122 people on board were lost.

Years later, in 1958, a fisherman called Bill Kirkpatrick found the wreck of the *SS Yongala* when his fishing line caught on something large on the seabed. Bill peered into the water with a glass-bottomed box and saw the top of the shipwreck below the surface.

The *SS Yongala* is now rated as one of the best wreck dives in the world. Every year, more than 10,000 divers come to visit the wreck. It is covered in so much sea life it can be hard to see that it was once a ship. But there are signs here and there, like the ship's masts and rudder—even a bath and toilets!

# MEET THE RESIDENTS

The most vibrant animals on the reef, and the easiest to spot, are fish. From huge shimmering shoals that waft around the coral, to tiny colorful individuals that dart between rocks and crevices, there are so many varieties to be explored.

*Butterflyfish*

*Angelfish*

*Dottybacks*

Parrotfish nibble seaweed using their beak-like front teeth. When they scrape up seaweed, they also swallow chunks of dead coral, which they grind down with a second set of teeth at the back of their throat. This coral comes out of the other end as sand. Most of the sand on many tropical beaches is actually parrotfish poop!

Damselfish tend reef "gardens" of seaweed. They get very angry if anyone tries to steal their prized crops and will chase off other fish no matter how big they are, while gnashing their teeth together, making a drumming sound. They will even chase after scuba divers!

# PLANTS OF THE REEF

Growing next to the reef are lush underwater meadows of seagrass, home to millions of tiny creatures. Seagrass leaves can grow up to five feet long, and they produce **pollen**, flowers, fruits, and seeds just like plants on land. The pollen float through the water or stick to the bodies of little animals, like worms and baby crabs, so that they can be carried to new places. These tiny pollen carriers are like the bees of the sea!

*Mangrove roots stick up from the water like snorkels, helping them breathe, and their crooked trunks keep them upright amongst crashing waves.*

*Young fish grow up on seagrass meadows and underwater mangrove forests before they move on to their final destination—the coral reef.*

## WHY TREES MATTER

Tree roots help to hold the soil together and stop it from washing onto the reef, where it blocks out precious sunlight. The roots also keep **pesticides** from farmland and other pollutants from getting to the reef. A lot of trees along the Australian coast have been cut down to make way for farms. Now, Aboriginal people, conservationists, and farmers are working hard to replant native trees and shrubs at the edges of the sea to help save the reef.

*Anemones*

## FLORA OR FAUNA?

Many reef animals are easy to mistake for plants or **fungi**. Coral boulders for example, are often covered in tiny worms called Christmas tree worms. They're the only animals in the world with eyes in their gills! They peep out from their burrows, ready to disappear at the first sign of danger. The reef is full of fantastic sea life in many shapes and forms.

*Christmas tree worm*

*Sausage-like sea cucumbers lie around, slurping up sand.*

## SIMPLE SPONGES

The reef is covered in goopy splotches, like rainbow-colored sneezes. Even these are animals! Aptly called sponges, they're like bags full of holes that spend their lives sucking in water and filtering microscopic scraps of food. They are prey for other animals, like the butterflyfish.

*Feather stars are related to starfish, but they have lots more legs.*

## HUNGRY STARFISH

One reef-dwelling creature that is a threat to its own home
is the crown of thorns starfish. The size of a car tire and covered
in hundreds of poisonous spines, it creeps onto corals, sticks
its stomach out through its mouth, and digests the living polyps.

One of these starfish can produce 65 million eggs a year, although many do not survive to adulthood. But after a flood or a storm, nutrients like fertilizers from farms get washed onto the reef. These chemicals feed plankton in the water, which in turn feed the starfish larvae, so more of them survive. This causes their numbers to explode and they cover the reef, killing huge areas of coral.

Divers try to control these outbreaks by killing as many starfish as possible. Killing starfish like this helps protect individual reefs, but there can be millions of them all along the Great Barrier Reef—far too many to kill one by one. To halt the starfish outbreaks, we need to keep the water as unpolluted as possible.

# SPINELESS SHELLS

**Mollusks** are soft and squashy on the inside and most of them have a hard protective covering on the outside called an exoskeleton—also known as a seashell.

## SHELL SUITS

Giant clams make the world's biggest seashells, and can weigh as much as two baby elephants. They spend their lives fixed firmly to the reef just like other **bivalve** mollusks, including oysters and mussels. Clams have hundreds of tiny eyes, which sense approaching predators so that they can snap shut and protect the soft body inside.

The cone snail sniffs for small fish or worms with its long **proboscis**, then shoots out teeth filled with poison and swallows its paralyzed prey whole.

Sea snails have one spiraling shell and creep around on a muscly foot.

## NEW MEDICINES

Scientists have found that the poisons in the teeth of cone snails are made up of hundreds of chemicals known as conotoxins. Each one has a particular effect, such as paralysis or sleep. By copying these powerful toxins in the lab, we can make new medicines, such as painkillers.

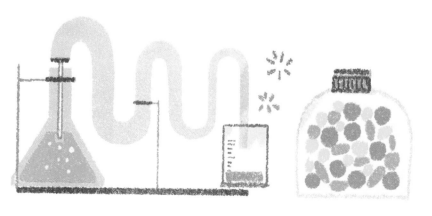

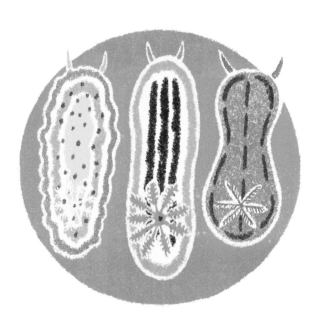

Sea slugs, also known as nudibranchs, are mollusks with no shells. They taste awful, and their stunning coloring warns predators to leave them alone.

# TENTACULAR WONDERS

Octopuses are also mollusks with no shells. These intelligent **cephalopods** have the biggest brains of any spineless creature and are **carnivorous**.

Half of an octopus's 500 million brain cells are located in their eight arms. So in a way their arms can think for themselves! Their sensitive suckers touch and taste, working out if something is worth grabbing and eating.

You might see an octopus carrying a coconut or an empty clam shell to use as a shelter, or it can camouflage itself by changing color and texture to match its surroundings and disappear right before your eyes!

Mimic octopuses living on the Great Barrier Reef do amazing impressions of lots of other animals, such as dangerous sea snakes and lionfish. This probably scares off other animals, which think twice about trying to eat them.

# CLAW CREW

More than a thousand crustacean species live on the Great Barrier Reef. Crustaceans are animals such as crabs, lobsters, and shrimp that have tough exoskeletons to protect them. Unlike mollusks, which only ever make one shell, most crustaceans shed theirs when they become too big and grow a new one. They have pinching claws, which can be regrown if they are damaged or bitten off by predators.

*Pom pom crabs look like cheerleaders. They pick up a stinging anemone in each claw and wave them around as weapons.*

*The mantis shrimp stuns its prey with a 45-mph punch— the world's fastest!*

## ALL CHANGE!

Unlike most crabs, hermit crabs have no exoskeletons, instead living inside empty seashells. When they grow too big for their shells, hermits meet up and form long lines, with the smallest crab at one end and the largest at the other. Everyone swaps shells with the next crab in line, and they all get a new shell of just the right size.

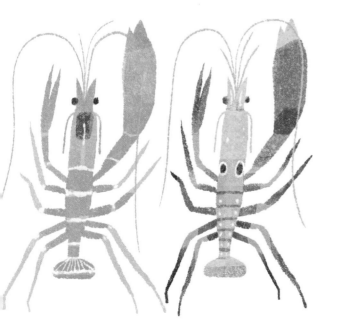

## SUPER SNAPPERS

A constant crackling sound on coral reefs is made by thousands of pistol shrimp. Each has one claw that is much bigger than the other. When the shrimp snaps the big claw shut, it makes bubbles that collapse with a loud pop. This releases a tiny flash of light, and for a split second the surrounding water heats up to almost 8,500°F—almost as hot as the surface of the sun! The shockwave can stun and kill small prey nearby.

# PARTNERSHIPS ON THE REEF

Tightly-packed creatures on the Great Barrier Reef get along by forming close partnerships. This is called **symbiosis**.

## ODD COUPLES

Clownfish hide from attackers among anemones' stinging tentacles, all the while wriggling and fidgeting, which draws in fresh, oxygen-rich water that anemones need to grow bigger. They also chase off butterflyfish that try to nibble the anemone's tentacles.

Small fish called gobies live in holes in the sand, along with their partners . . . shrimp! Shrimp can't see very well, so they are in charge of cleaning the burrow while the goby stands guard at the entrance, watching for danger.

## CLEANING SERVICE

Some fish get their food from cleaning other creatures. The tiny cleaner wrasse swims right inside the mouth of a huge grouper, but the grouper doesn't snap its jaws shut. Instead, it stays perfectly still while the little fish cleans its teeth. The brave little wrasse nibbles dead skin, scales, and blood-sucking **parasites** from all the other fish on the reef, keeping them clean and healthy.

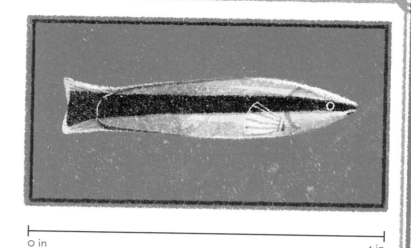

0 in                                    4 in

*Cleaner wrasse*

# NIGHTTIME ON THE REEF

When darkness falls on the reef, daytime fish such as angelfish and butterflyfish find caves and crevices to hide in. Parrotfish make themselves a sleeping bag from a bubble of sticky, foul-smelling goo to repel lurking parasites. But you'd be mistaken to believe that the reef transforms into a peaceful and quiet habitat. Nighttime is often the most active time.

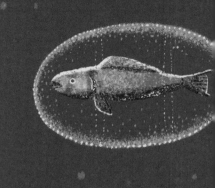

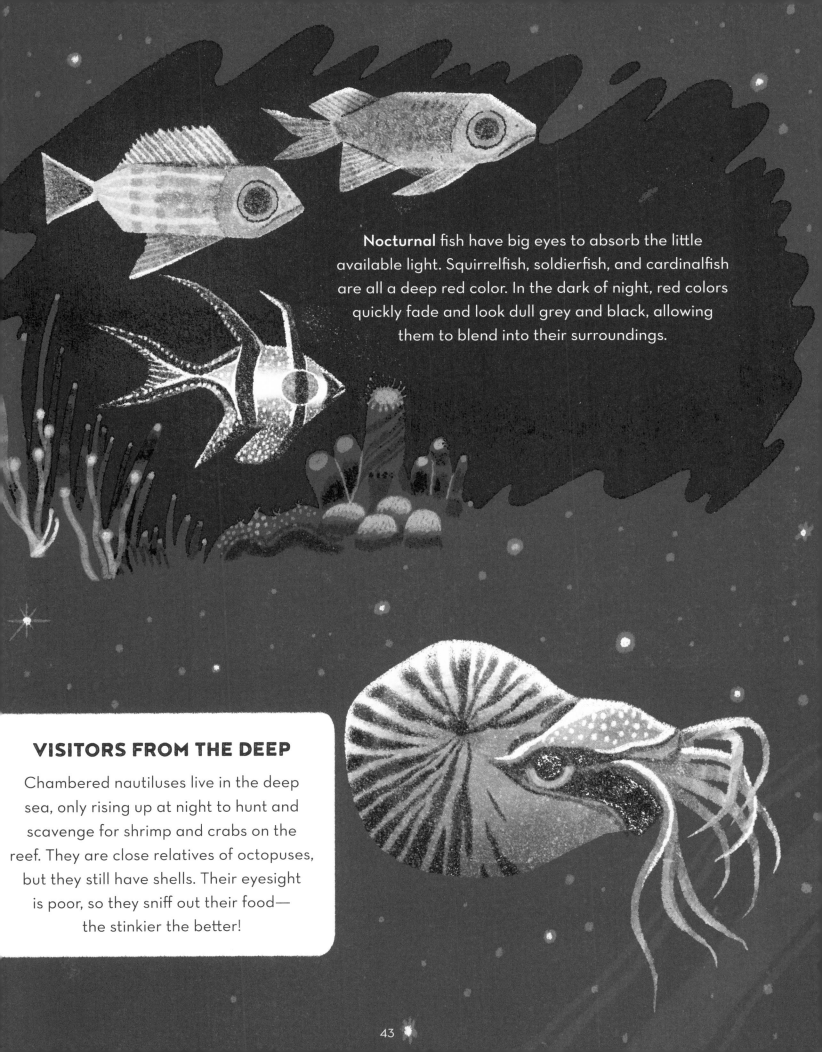

Nocturnal fish have big eyes to absorb the little available light. Squirrelfish, soldierfish, and cardinalfish are all a deep red color. In the dark of night, red colors quickly fade and look dull grey and black, allowing them to blend into their surroundings.

## VISITORS FROM THE DEEP

Chambered nautiluses live in the deep sea, only rising up at night to hunt and scavenge for shrimp and crabs on the reef. They are close relatives of octopuses, but they still have shells. Their eyesight is poor, so they sniff out their food— the stinkier the better!

# NEIGHBORS OF THE REEF

# SHARKS AND RAYS

All of the fish we've met so far on the reef are bony fish—their skeletons are made of hard bone, like your legs and arms. Other fish have bendy skeletons made of cartilage, the same stuff that makes up your ears and the end of your nose. These are sharks and rays. From fearsome giants like tiger and bull sharks, to wobbegongs and epaulettes, which don't look much like sharks at all, there is plenty of variety to be found on the reef.

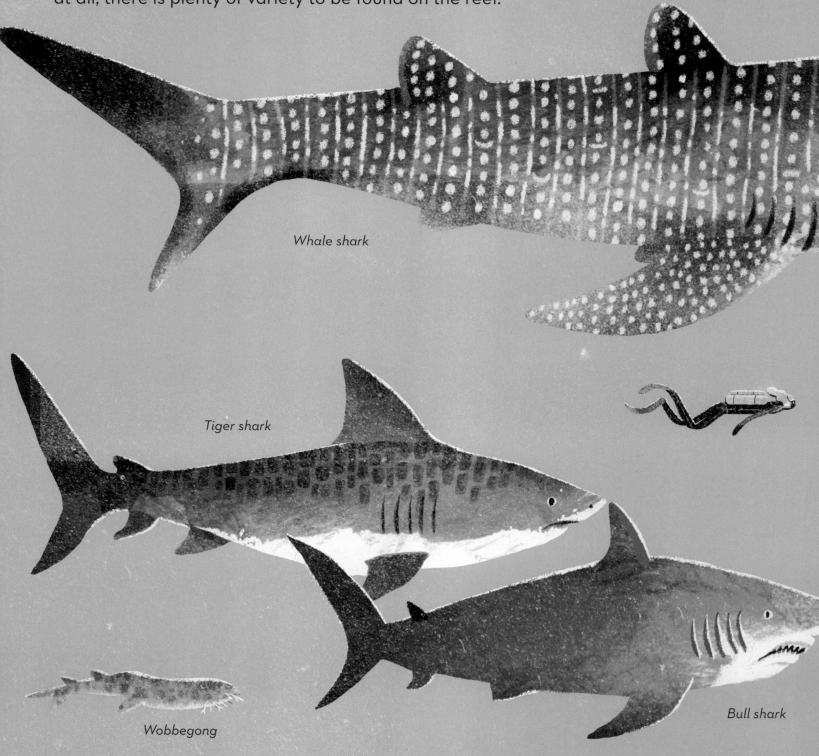

*Whale shark*

*Tiger shark*

*Wobbegong*

*Bull shark*

Grey reef shark

Epaulette shark

Blacktip reef shark

Whitetip reef shark

## LIVING A FLAT LIFE

Rays are the sharks' flattened cousins. A stingray looks like a pancake
with a long tail and a sting at the end, and while sharks have gills
on the sides of their bodies, rays always have gills underneath.
Eagle rays and manta rays flap their triangular fins like
huge birds flying through the water.

Stingray

# MARINE MAMMALS

Cetaceans are ocean mammals such as whales and dolphins. At least thirty cetacean species live on and around the Great Barrier Reef. Migaloo is the world's most famous whale—an **albino** humpback male who has been regularly spotted around the reef for over twenty years.

*Dwarf minke whale*

*Humpback whale*

## CATCHY TUNES

Humpback whales spend the summer in Antarctica, gorging on **krill**. Each winter, these huge whales arrive at the Great Barrier Reef to mate and give birth in warmer waters. Male humpbacks sing beautiful songs of clicks, squeals, and squeaks, which they pass on to other whales. It's like a whale radio station! Eventually, whales thousands of miles away sing the same tune.

For some whales and dolphins, these noises serve another purpose as well—echolocation. They make pulses of sound and listen for echoes bouncing back, then use their brains to decipher these echoes. This way, these cetaceans can figure out how close they are to other creatures and underwater structures, even when they can't see anything.

Humpback dolphin

Bottlenose dolphin

Snubfin dolphin

## GRASS LOVERS

Herds of dugongs swim along the reef. They have tiny eyes and don't see well, but whiskers on their snouts help them find tasty clumps of seagrass. Unlike whales, which can stay underwater for an hour or longer, dugongs only hold their breath for a minute or two at most.

Dugongs

# TAILS WITH SCALES

If you thought you'd only find fish and marine mammals on the reef, think again. The diversity and unique conditions found here mean that the reef attracts some unusual reptilian visitors too.

## SLITHERING SWIMMERS

Sea snakes have flattened tails for swimming, but still breathe air like their land-dwelling cousins. Their lungs reach almost to the end of their bodies and can hold enough air for them to stay underwater for up to two hours at a time. All fourteen species of sea snakes living on the Great Barrier Reef give birth to live young in the water.

## CREEPING CROCS

Enormous saltwater crocodiles lurk on beaches and among mangroves along the Great Barrier Reef. These giant reptiles can grow up to twenty-three feet long, and have the strongest bite of any animal.

# TURTLE TERRITORY

Six of the world's seven sea turtle species live around the Great Barrier Reef. Female sea turtles have an internal compass which lets them sense the Earth's **magnetic fields**. This helps them navigate the oceans to find their way back to the very beach where they were hatched, to lay their eggs. When they are finished, they shuffle back to the sea. The hatchlings will do the same when they emerge from the sand a month later.

*Leatherback turtle*
*(the world's biggest species)*

*Hawksbill turtle*

*Flatback turtle*

Loggerhead turtle

Green turtle

Olive ridley turtle
(the world's smallest species)

## TEMPERATURE TROUBLES

Turtles on the Great Barrier Reef are also suffering from climate change. This is because temperature determines the sex of baby turtles—if the nest is under 81°F all the eggs hatch as males, if it is above 87°F they will all be female. At temperatures in between, there's a mixture of males and females. At present, only one per cent of green turtles hatching on the Great Barrier Reef are males. If temperatures keep rising, there may no longer be enough males to mate with all the females and the population could decline.

# FLYING VISITORS

Many islands on the Great Barrier Reef started as big, empty piles of sand made of parrotfish poop. Then, later on, seeds arrived in the droppings of visiting birds, which grew into creeping vines with colorful flowers and clumps of spiky spinifex grass. This vegetation encouraged more birds to visit, filling the sky with squawks and flapping wings.

The tiny reef island of Michaelmas Cay is home to thousands of birds building nests and raising their fluffy chicks. Here are some examples of the common birds that nest there.

*Sooty tern*

*Common or brown noddy*

*Brown booby*

54

## BOASTING BIRDS

Frigatebirds can fly for years across the seas. The only time
frigatebirds come to land is to find mates. Many fly to Michaelmas Cay,
where the males put on a bizarre display. They inflate a bright red pouch
on their throats, which they wobble and vibrate at passing females.
This is the frigatebird way of saying, "I am definitely the best mate here!"

# A HUMAN HABITAT

# HARMONIOUS HUNTERS

If we traveled back in time thousands of years we'd meet people living along the coast of Australia and on the islands of the Great Barrier Reef. These people, the first who came to live here, are known as the Aborigines and Torres Strait Islanders. They relied on the reef and its islands for everything they needed. They ventured out across the reef in wooden canoes to fish and hunt, and built stone walls on the seabed to trap fish when the tide dropped.

Aborigines and Torres Strait Islanders harvested and hunted reef-dwelling animals for thousands of years without damaging wild populations. They understood to leave them alone at certain places and times, so that there were always more in the future.

Today, these people don't tend to live where their ancestors did, because many were forced out to other places in Australia by European settlers. But the clans keep strong bonds with the reef and they still have rights to fish and hunt there. Instead of wooden canoes, many now use boats with engines, and they hunt using modern fishing rods and spear guns. Despite this, they still use their ancestors' knowledge to find animals and decide where they're allowed to go. This is how the Aborigines and Torres Straight Islanders keep their cultures alive and continue to teach young people their stories and traditions.

# LEGENDARY TALES

There are currently more than seventy different groups of Aborigines and Torres Strait Islanders. Each Aboriginal clan has its own language, and they all tell stories of The Dreamtime. This is a spiritual belief about how the world was made and how people can find sacred places and food. We know these stories today because they've been passed down from generation to generation. Some are secret stories, kept within clans, and some have been told to the public with permission of the storytellers.

## NO FISHING ALLOWED

Two boys got in trouble when they fished where they weren't supposed to. There was a forbidden place on the water that was home to a huge shovelnose ray known as Dhui Dhui. When the boys let down their line, Dhui Dhui grabbed it and towed the boat out beyond the horizon, where the boys joined the stars. The story says the constellation called the Southern Cross is Dhui Dhui, and the two pointer stars are the boys.

# OF SHARKS AND STINGRAYS

A father and son were swept from their boat and got stuck out on the reef. They waited all night to be rescued, while sharks swam around and brushed past their legs. But the creatures never attacked them. The clan that tells this story believes the man and his son stayed safe because the shark is their totem, an animal that serves as the symbol of a clan.

# NEW ARRIVALS

In 1770, Captain James Cook arrived on his ship *HMS Endeavour* and claimed Australia for Great Britain. His famous voyage also resulted in his accidentally discovering the Great Barrier Reef, when his ship crashed into it on a June night. At first, Captain Cook and his crew were baffled as to how they could have run aground in seemingly open waters, and were forced to throw many of their belongings into the sea in order to float the ship and save themselves. They were astonished to find what lay beneath.

## NEW PROBLEMS

*HMS Endeavour* was not the only ship to have explored this coast. Unfortunately, when other Europeans arrived, they realized they could make lots of money from the Great Barrier Reef. Divers picked sea cucumbers off the seabed and sold them to China, where they are considered a delicacy. Tens of thousands of turtles were hunted for their shells to make ornaments and for their meat. The European settlers also gathered millions of oysters, mostly to cut circles from their shiny shells and make buttons. They didn't control or limit what they took. But by the twentieth century, people realized that the reef's animals were disappearing and needed protection.

*The exact location where Captain Cook crashed into the reef is now known as Endeavour Reef. There's no shipwreck to see there—Captain Cook and his men fixed the hole in the ship and sailed north.*

# LIVING IN HARMONY

Humans have lived on and beside the Great Barrier Reef ever since it formed thousands of years ago. Over time, we've learned much about it, and its inhabitants, and how we can share the environment together.

## SIGNS ON THE REEF

Aboriginal people learned the changes that take place throughout the year on the reef, and knew which signs told them to expect different things. For instance, when the first thunderstorm came each year, or when the first pigeons flew through the sky, they knew it was a good time to hunt for stingrays.

## REEF TOOLS

In the past, people used animals from the reef for all sorts of resources besides food. They took sharp spines from stingray tails and made them into spear tips, and carved seashells into hooks to catch fish. Rough shark skin was used as sandpaper to smooth down wooden carvings, and sharks' teeth were used to scratch patterns into them. Nowadays we use different materials, or source them sustainably.

## SACRED ANIMALS

People from different Aboriginal clans along the coast each had their own special animal for a totem. This could be a crocodile, a pelican, a shark, or maybe an octopus. In some clans it was forbidden to hunt and eat the totem animal. Some clans gave every child their own totem and carved it into a pendant for them.

# REEF ART

As sacred thousands of years ago as it still is today, the Great Barrier Reef was a valued source of inspiration to its inhabitants. They expressed all that they witnessed through vibrant paintings and carefully sculpted masks, which can still be seen today.

## ROCK ART

The oldest rock art found in Australia dates back 28,000 years. Some of the most spectacular are on Yindayin Island, several hours' sail from mainland Australia. Up the island's stony paths is an overhanging rock face covered in hundreds of pictures—stingrays, crocodiles, turtles, dugongs, and lots of boats.

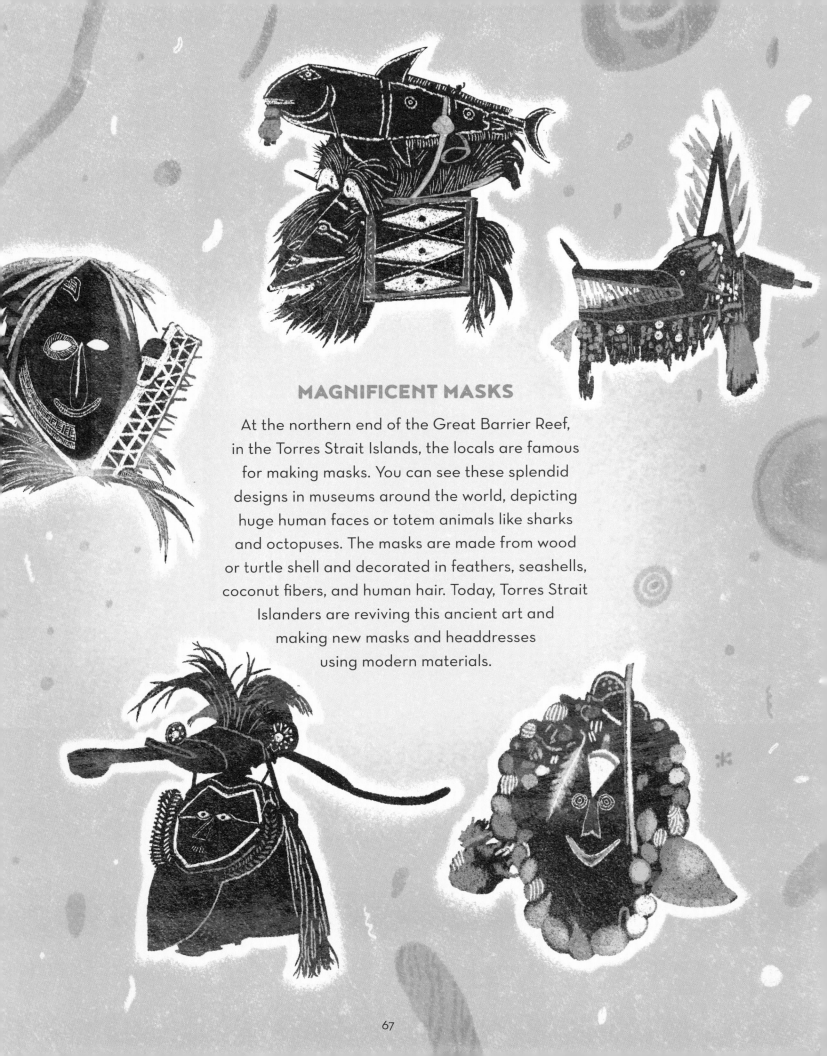

## MAGNIFICENT MASKS

At the northern end of the Great Barrier Reef, in the Torres Strait Islands, the locals are famous for making masks. You can see these splendid designs in museums around the world, depicting huge human faces or totem animals like sharks and octopuses. The masks are made from wood or turtle shell and decorated in feathers, seashells, coconut fibers, and human hair. Today, Torres Strait Islanders are reviving this ancient art and making new masks and headdresses using modern materials.

# A NEW DAWN

# IN HOT WATER

The single biggest worry for the Great Barrier Reef is the fact that the sea is getting warmer. Most scientists agree on that. When corals get hot, they get stressed and spit out their zoox. Without them, corals become transparent, and the reef turns ghostly white. This is called coral bleaching. It's not just their colors that are lost, but most of their food too, and so they begin to starve. Due to recent climate change, this has already happened on the Great Barrier Reef in 2016 and 2017, then again in 2020.

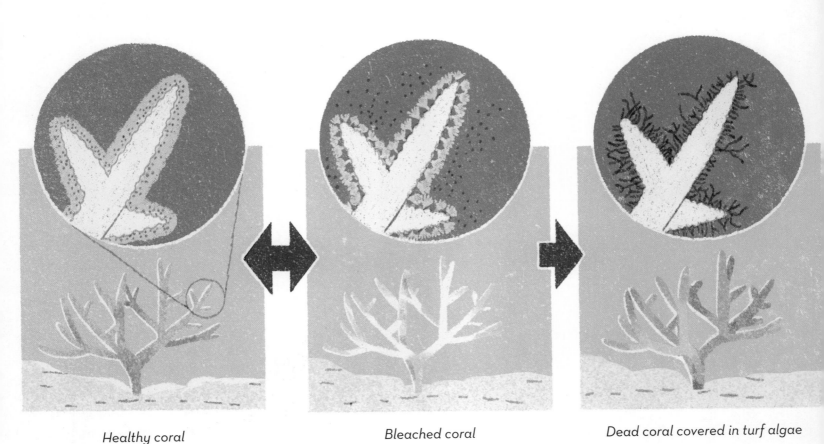

Healthy coral

Bleached coral

Dead coral covered in turf algae

## TERRY HUGHES

Terry is a scientist who specializes in coral bleaching. He led a team who used helicopters and small airplanes to fly up and down the reef, taking photographs of the white areas to measure how much had bleached.

Climate change is largely caused by the burning of **fossils fuels** like gasoline and coal. These activities release carbon dioxide into the air, trapping the sun's heat and warming the planet and its oceans.

Around a quarter of carbon dioxide emissions dissolve in the oceans, causing what is known as ocean acidification. As seawater becomes more acidic, it makes life difficult for marine animals with chalky shells and exoskeletons, like mollusks and corals. Coral polyps struggle to get enough chemical building blocks, called ions, to make their exoskeletons, and they begin to melt away.

# THE PROBLEM OF PLASTIC

When you throw things in the garbage or flush them down the toilet, they often end up in the sea. Plastic trash can hang around for hundreds of years without completely breaking down. Every minute, the equivalent of a truck's worth of plastic waste is dumped in the sea and a lot of it reaches coral reefs.

## PLASTIC SEAS

Plastic can be covered in microbes like **bacteria** and **viruses**, which make corals sick. Infected corals turn strange colors and get nasty-looking spots, and often they can die. Microplastics are also formed when larger chunks of plastic break apart or when synthetic fibers wash out of our clothes. Corals can eat these tiny pieces, which then clog up their stomachs.

## SAY NO TO PLASTIC

People around the world buy a million plastic bottles every minute! If more of us used refillable bottles, much less plastic would pollute the sea. Next time you go shopping for clothes, you can also look at the labels to find things made with natural fibers like cotton and wool instead of synthetic materials like nylon and polyester. We can all take reusable bags to the grocery store and say no to plastic straws in our drinks and single-use plastic packaging.

# FATES INTERTWINED

When the reef is in trouble, so are its human neighbors. As the oceans warm, melting glaciers and ice sheets release more water into the sea and so the water level rises. The corals become so stressed from the warm and acidic water that they may not grow fast enough to keep up with these rising seas. Without high reefs, ocean waves will roll right on to the beaches, washing away sand and threatening people's homes.

To stop the seas getting warmer and more acidic, we need to stop burning fossil fuels and reduce our **carbon footprints**. We can walk, cycle, or take the train instead of driving or flying everywhere, and we can eat food that's grown locally and not flown in from other countries.

## GIVING UP FOSSIL FUEL

Many people are angry with the Australian government for planning to build a huge coal mine and port right next to the Great Barrier Reef, stirring up mud, and creating more pollution in the sea. Burning coal will also release more carbon dioxide, making things even worse.

But it doesn't have to be this way. We could leave fossil fuels in the ground and use other power sources. "Green energy," also known as renewable energy, harnesses power from the sun, wind, and waves, and releases far less carbon dioxide. We already know how to do this by building energy generators such as solar panels and wind turbines. What we really need now is for politicians and big companies around the world to take climate change seriously and invest in renewable energy.

## OCEAN-FRIENDLY SEAFOOD

Saving the Great Barrier Reef means saving plants and other animals too. Fish like parrotfish munch seaweeds and stop them from overgrowing and killing the corals. Today, if you eat fish and other sea creatures, you can choose not to eat seaweed munchers like parrotfish, and only eat fish that are caught sustainably.

# SAVING THE REEF

There are lots of brilliant scientists and inventors who are fighting to save the reef. They are testing different technologies to try and help the endangered corals become stronger.

## CATCHING CORALS

To try and fight coral bleaching, some teams of divers are collecting bags of fertilized coral eggs during those times when the reef explodes into a huge, colorful snowstorm. They then release those eggs in areas where corals have died from bleaching. The hope is that the coral larvae will settle down and grow into new colonies, helping the reef to regrow.

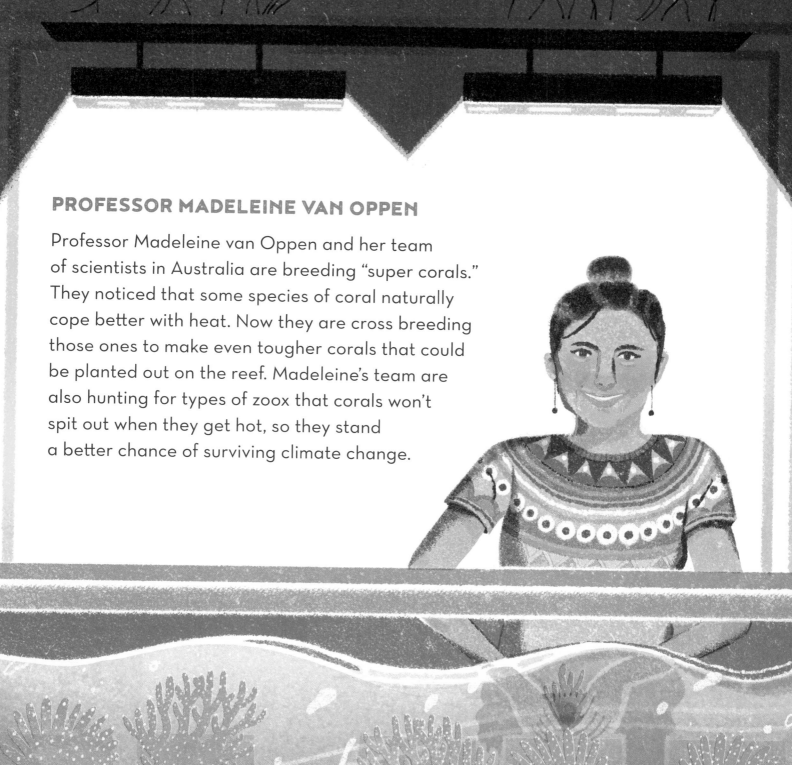

## PROFESSOR MADELEINE VAN OPPEN

Professor Madeleine van Oppen and her team of scientists in Australia are breeding "super corals." They noticed that some species of coral naturally cope better with heat. Now they are cross breeding those ones to make even tougher corals that could be planted out on the reef. Madeleine's team are also hunting for types of zoox that corals won't spit out when they get hot, so they stand a better chance of surviving climate change.

# OUR SHARED TREASURE

The future of the reef also depends on the next generation of people who will study it. We need people to identify its problems, find solutions, and enforce rules to keep it protected. Perhaps one of those people will be you!

## WHY PROTECT THE REEF?

It's often said that the main reason to save the Great Barrier Reef is because it's worth so much money— it's been valued at 56 billion Australian dollars, mostly from the money tourists pay to visit. But can we really put a price on this amazing place? The Great Barrier Reef is irreplaceable. There's simply nowhere else like it. Surely, that's worth more than anything money can buy.

Hopefully in years to come, this awesome maze of life will still exist, full of angelfish, butterflyfish, corals, clownfish, dolphins, dugongs, sea snakes, seahorses, turtles, whales, and everything else that makes the Great Barrier Reef one of the greatest wonders on Earth.

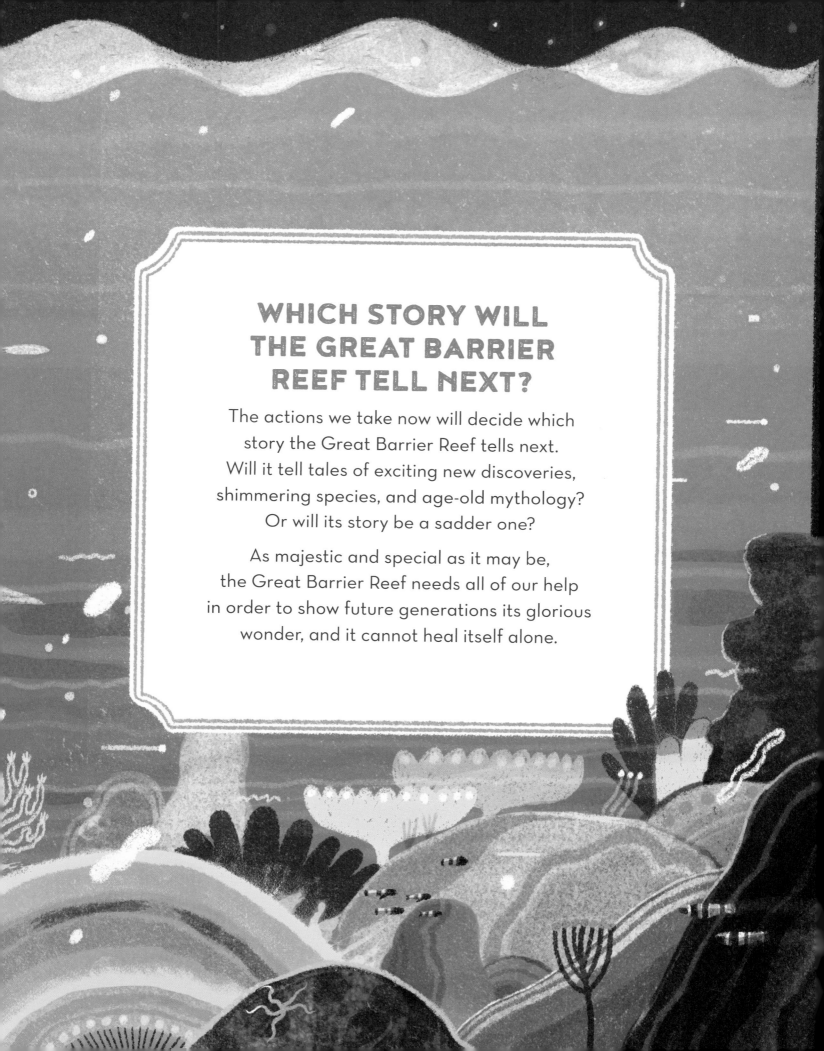

# WHICH STORY WILL THE GREAT BARRIER REEF TELL NEXT?

The actions we take now will decide which story the Great Barrier Reef tells next. Will it tell tales of exciting new discoveries, shimmering species, and age-old mythology? Or will its story be a sadder one?

As majestic and special as it may be, the Great Barrier Reef needs all of our help in order to show future generations its glorious wonder, and it cannot heal itself alone.

# GLOSSARY

**Albino** Person or animal that has missing skin pigments, and so appears light-colored or even completely white.

**Bacteria** Living thing made up of a single cell, which can often cause disease.

**bivalve** Type of mollusk with a two-part shell that is connected with a hinge.

**buoyancy** Ability of an object to float.

**Carbon footprint** Amount of carbon dioxide someone or something produces.

**carnivore** Animal that preys on other animals.

**cephalopod** Type of mollusk with arms or tentacles.

**coral bleaching** Process where polyps leave a coral, making it become less colorful.

**Echolocation** Process where an animal sends out sounds and listens for echoes to map the area around it.

**exoskeleton** Hard outer shell, found on some invertebrates (animals that do not have a backbone).

**Fossil fuel** Natural substance like coal or gas, which we burn for fuel.

**fungi** Type of living thing, such as mushrooms or mold, which feeds on decaying matter to survive.

**Krill** Small crustaceans that are types of plankton.

**Larvae** Tiny, young stages of many aquatic animals, including corals, fish, and starfish. They drift or swim around. They usually look very different to the adults.

**Magnetic field** An invisible force created by forces inside of the earth.

**microscope** Scientific instrument that lets people view things that would ordinarily be too small to see.

**mollusk** A category of spineless animals, most of which live inside shells.

**Nocturnal** Describes a creature which is most active at night and usually sleeps during the day.

**Oxygen** The gas which makes up 21% of the air we breathe, which life needs to survive.

**Parasite** Living thing that lives on or inside another living thing.

**pesticides** Chemical used to kill insects and pests that eat farmers' crops.

**plankton** Minute creatures that live in the water, either animals called zooplankton or plant-like organisms called phytoplankton. Both types are eaten by lots of animals.

**pollen** A substance produced by plants, allowing them to reproduce.

**polyp** One of the tiny animals that make up coral colonies.

**proboscis** Long, nose-like structure on an animal.

**Sonar** Technology that uses sound to detect objects on or under the surface of the water.

**symbiosis** Close relationship between two living things of different species, which benefits each in a different way.

**Virus** Tiny particles that can cause disease.

**Zooxanthellae** Tiny creatures that live inside coral polyps and get their energy from the sun. "Zoox" for short.

# INDEX

# NOTES AND IDEAS FOR TEACHERS

**S** TEACHER RESOURCES
Prepared by SHAPES for Schools

## TOPIC 1: WHAT IS CORAL?

- How many species of coral live on the Great Barrier Reef?

- What is a polyp?

- How many polyps make up a colony?

- In what ways are polyps similar to jellyfish? Or to plants?

- What do polyps do at night-time?

- Having read page 15, turn to look at the front cover of the book. Which different types of coral can you identify on the front cover?

- Would you like to visit the coral reef? Why?

- What do you think the divers on page 14 can see? What do you think might they be thinking or feeling?

### ACTIVITY:

Imagine you have just been on your very first dive exploring the Great Barrier Reef! What did you see? How did it feel to be amongst one of the greatest natural wonders of the world?

Write an email home to a friend telling them all about your experience. Use descriptive language to help them imagine the amazing reef environment.

Tip: Learn more about diving on pages 18–19.

# TOPIC 2: RESIDENTS OF THE REEF

- What do you think the word "vibrant" means?
- Do you know what a "shoal" is?
- Can you find two verbs on page 28 that describe how fish move?
- What do you think the Butterflyfish might use its long snout for?

**ACTIVITY:**

Choose a species of fish that lives in the reef (see pages 28-29 and 42-43). Find out its size, what it eats, and a fun fact about it. Then, go outside, draw a picture to scale on the playground, and take a tour of the reef! With your class, imagine you're on a sailing boat, and when the group spots your fish, it's your turn to teach your classmates.

- How is the Parrotfish well adapted to its environment?
- Why do you think Parrotfish is named the "Parrotfish?"
- What might the diver in the illustration on page 29 be thinking?
- Which species of fish would you most like to see if you visited the Great Barrier Reef?

# TOPIC 3: REEF ART

- What do you think the word "sacred" means?
- How many years ago were the rock paintings on Yindayin Island created?
- Do you know what life was like where you live at the time when the rock paintings were created on Yindayin Island?
- Why do you think the ancient inhabitants of Yindayin Island might have created the rock art?

- How do you think these ancient people felt about the Great Barrier Reef?
- What might the ancient inhabitants of the island have had in common with modern day people?
- What materials are the Torres Strait Island masks made from?
- What animals can you see in the illustrations of the Torres Strait Island masks?

**ACTIVITY:**

Create your own piece of art inspired by the Great Barrier Reef. Look at Lisk Feng's stunning illustrations, and look online for photos of the Yindayin Island rock paintings and Torres Strait Island masks to remind you that people have been inspired by this underwater wonderland for many thousands of years!

Why not hold an exhibition and invite friends and family to come and enjoy your reef-inspired art?

# TOPIC 4: PROTECTING THE REEF

| Why should we protect the Great Barrier Reef? | What threats does the Great Barrier Reef face? | What actions can we take to protect the Great Barrier Reef? |
| --- | --- | --- |
| | | |

**ACTIVITY:**

Create a leaflet to inform people about the threats the Great Barrier Reef faces and inspire them to help protect it.

First, copy the table above. Read to the end of the book and make notes in your table. Use your notes to plan and write your leaflet. To make your leaflet clear and grab your reader's attention, you could include a bold title, diagrams, and lists. When you have finished, display your leaflet for visitors to your school to read, or share it with friends and family!

- How does plastic in the ocean affect the corals?

- Can you give three ways that people can "say no to plastic?"

- How do you feel when you think about the threats to the Great Barrier Reef?

- Can you think of one thing you could try to do to help protect the Great Barrier Reef?

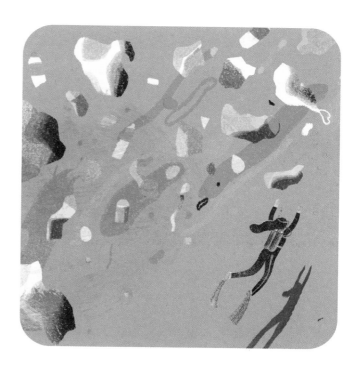

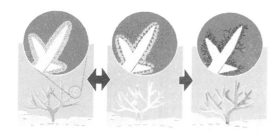

- What happens when corals get hot?

- How does the burning of fossil fuels cause the planet and its oceans to heat up?

- What happens when carbon dioxide dissolves in the oceans?

- What plastic items can you see in the illustration on pages 74–75?

Download these worksheets online

## WRITTEN BY DR HELEN SCALES

Dr Helen Scales is a marine biologist who has studied many parts of the oceans, from coral reefs in Borneo to mangroves in Madagascar. She got to know the Great Barrier Reef working as a dive master, introducing other scuba divers to its living wonders. Helen writes books and articles, makes radio programs, teaches at Cambridge University, and advises the charity Sea Changers, which protects British sea life. She lives in Cambridge, UK and on the Atlantic coast of France.

## ILLUSTRATED BY LISK FENG

Lisk Feng is an award-winning illustrator from China, now based in New York. She has worked on projects with clients such as *The New Yorker*, Apple, Penguin, Airbnb, *The New York Times*, and Chanel. Her work has received awards such as the Society of Illustrators Silver Medal, Communication Arts Excellence Award, and 3X3 Silver Medal. She was awarded one of the Forbes "30 under 30" on the Art and Style list in 2019, and the Bologna Ragazzi Award for the book *Everest* with Flying Eye Books in 2019.

## ALSO IN THE SERIES

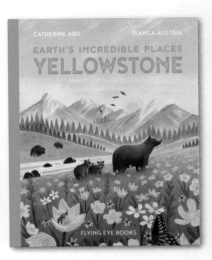